Let Us Have Music for Piano

Seventy Four Famous Melodies

ARRANGED AND EDITED BY MAXWELL ECKSTEIN

CARL FISCHER®
62 Cooper Square, New York, NY 10003

Copyright © 1940 by Carl Fischer, Inc.
International Copyright Secured.
All rights reserved including performing rights.
WARNING! This publication is protected by Copyright law. To photocopy or reproduce by
any means is an infringement of the Copyright law. Anyone who reproduces copyrighted
matter is subject to substantial penalties and assessments for each infringement.
Printed in the U.S.A.

O2942

ISBN 0-8258-0047-1

Copyright 1940
by
CARL FISCHER, INC.
New York

International Copyright Secured

PRINTED IN U.S.A.

FOREWORD

These volumes have been prepared with the following points in view:

1. For adults or children who have a limited technique, and are in the early grades of piano playing.
2. For study and recreational purposes.
3. For sight reading.

The compositions herein are too difficult in their original form to be played by persons whose technical development is immature. They have therefore been carefully arranged in the easier keys, within the average vocal range, and are suitable for singing if desired, lyrics having been included with most of them. They have been edited to meet a specific need for elementary piano material.

We feel certain that this book will prove a valuable addition to the repertories of all who wish to make the music hour a pleasant one.

Maxwell Eckstein

ALPHABETICAL INDEX

Adeste Fideles. *Reading*	84
Aloha Oe! *Liliuokalani*	97
America. *Carey*	5
America, the Beautiful. *Ward*	6
Annie Laurie. *Scott*	61
Arkansas Traveler. *American*	13
Auld Lang Syne. *Scotch*	59
Ave Maria. *Schubert*	87
Battle Hymn of the Republic. *Bishop*	12
Beautiful Dreamer. *Foster*	33
Beautiful Heaven. *Mexican*	57
Blue Bells of Scotland, The. *Scotch*	60
Blue Danube. *Strauss*	80
Carry Me Back to Old Virginny. *Bland*	14
Comin' Thro' the Rye. *Scotch*	62
Country Gardens. *English*	40
Cradle Song. *Brahms*	96
Dark Eyes. *Russian*	72
Dixie. *Emmett*	10
Drink to Me Only with Thine Eyes. *English*	39
El Choclo. *Villoldo*	54
Flowers That Bloom in the Spring, The. *Sullivan*	52
Home on the Range. *American*	18
Home, Sweet Home. *Bishop*	22
Humoresque. *Dvorak*	98
I Am the Captain of the Pinafore. *Sullivan*	50
I'll Take You Home Again, Kathleen. *Westendorf*	20
I'm Called Little Buttercup. *Sullivan*	48
Jeanie with the Light Brown Hair. *Foster*	34
Juanita. *Spanish*	56
La Cucaracha. *Mexican*	58
La Donna e mobile. *Verdi*	86
La Marseillaise. *French*	110
Last Rose of Summer, The. *Irish*	64
Liebesträume. *Liszt*	92
Londonderry Air. *Irish*	63
Long, Long Ago. *Bayly*	24
Lost Chord, The. *Sullivan*	45
Love's Old Sweet Song. *Molloy*	25
Marche Slave. *Tschaikowsky*	76
Melody in F. *Rubinstein*	74
Merry Widow, The. *Lehar*	77
My Old Kentucky Home. *Foster*	30
Nearer My God to Thee. *Mason*	82
None But the Lonely Heart. *Tschaikowsky*	66
O Sole Mio. *Capua*	106
Oh, My Darling Clementine. *Montrose*	28
Oh! Susanna. *Foster*	29
Old Black Joe. *Foster*	35
Old Folks at Home. *Foster*	32
Old Oaken Bucket, The. *Kiallmark*	19
Old Refrain, The. *Viennese*	102
Poem. *Fibich*	108
Polly Wolly Doodle. *Traditional*	44
Pop Goes the Weasel. *American*	42
Rock of Ages. *Hastings*	83
Serenade. *Schubert*	94
Short'nin' Bread. *American*	38
Silent Night. *Gruber*	85
Silver Threads Among the Gold. *Danks*	26
Song of India, A. *Rimsky-Korsakoff*	70
Song of the Volga Boatmen. *Russian*	73
Songs My Mother Taught Me. *Dvorak*	100
Star-Spangled Banner, The. *Smith*	8
Stein Song. *Fenstad*	104
Swing Low, Sweet Chariot. *Spiritual*	36
Tales from the Vienna Woods. *Strauss*	78
Three Blind Mice. *Round*	43
Tit-Willow. *Sullivan*	53
Turkey in the Straw. *American*	16
Two Guitars. *Russian*	68
Volga Boatmen, Song of the. *Russian*	73
We Sail the Ocean Blue. *Sullivan*	46
Who Is Sylvia? *Schubert*	90
Yankee Doodle. *American*	9

Classified Index on Page 112

America
(My Country, 'Tis of Thee)

My country, 'tis of thee,
Sweet land of liberty,
Of thee I sing.
Land where my fathers died!
Land of the Pilgrims' pride!
From every mountainside,
Let freedom ring!

Our fathers' God, to Thee,
Author of liberty,
To Thee we sing.
Long may our land be bright
With freedom's holy light;
Protect us by Thy might,
Great God, our King!

HENRY CAREY (1685?-1743)
Arranged by Maxwell Eckstein

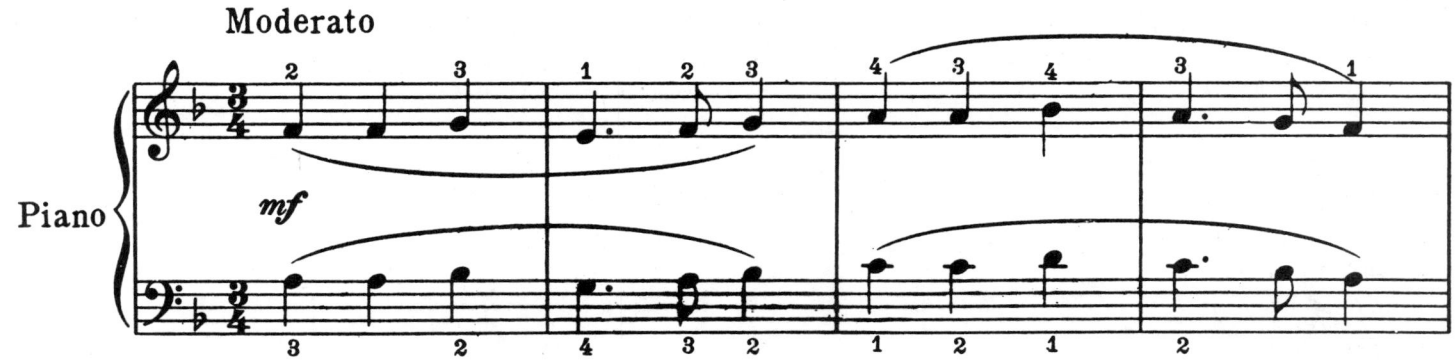

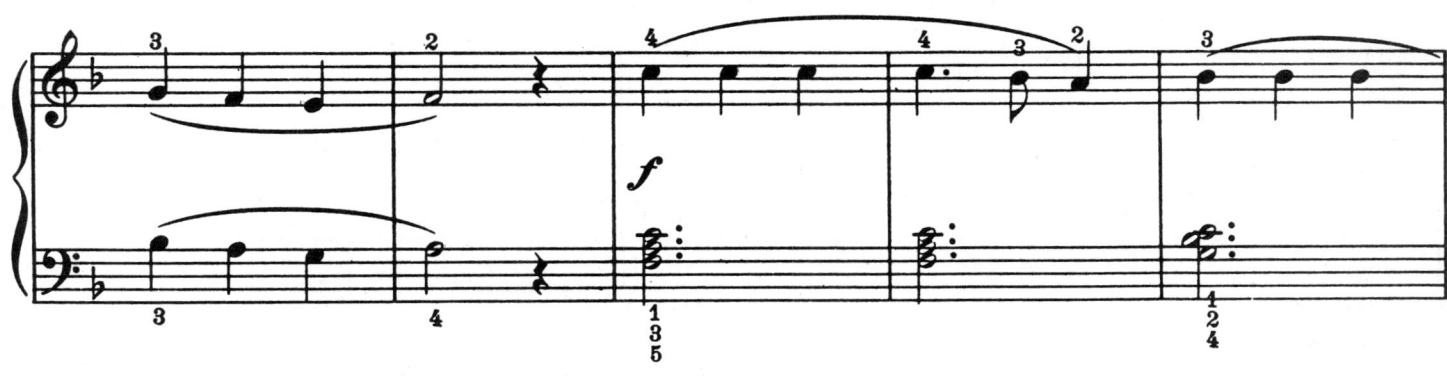

America, the Beautiful

O beautiful for spacious skies,
For amber waves of grain,
For purple mountain majesties
Above the fruited plain.
America! America! God shed His grace on thee,
And crown thy good with brotherhood
From sea to shining sea.

O beautiful for patriot dream
That sees beyond the years,
Thine alabaster cities gleam
Undimmed by human tears;
America! America! God shed His grace on thee,
And crown thy good with brotherhood
From sea to shining sea.

(Katharine Lee Bates)

SAMUEL A. WARD
Arranged by Maxwell Eckstein

The Star-Spangled Banner

Oh, say, can you see, by the dawn's early light,
What so proudly we hailed at the twilight's last gleaming?
Whose broad stripes and bright stars, thru the perilous fight,
O'er the ramparts we watched, were so gallantly streaming?
And the rockets' red glare, the bombs bursting in air,
Gave proof thru the night that our flag was still there.
Oh, say, does that Star-Spangled Banner yet wave
O'er the land of the free and the home of the brave?
(Francis Scott Key)

American National Anthem
J. S. SMITH (1750-1836)
Arranged by Maxwell Eckstein

Yankee Doodle

Fath'r and I went down to camp,
Along with Captain Good'in,
And there we saw the men and boys
As thick as hasty puddin'.

Chorus
Yankee Doodle, keep it up,
Yankee Doodle dandy,
Mind the music and the step,
And with the girls be handy.

And there we saw a thousand men,
As rich as Squire David;
And what they wasted every day,
I wish it could be saved,

And there was Captain Washington,
Upon a slapping stallion,
A-giving orders to his men;
I guess there was a million.

Arranged by Maxwell Eckstein

Dixie

I wish I was in de land ob cotton,
Old times dar am not forgotten,
Look away! Look away! Look away! Dixie Land.
In Dixie Land whar I was born in,
Early on one frosty mornin',
Look away! Look away! Look away! Dixie Land.
Den I wish I was in Dixie, Hooray! Hooray!
In Dixie Land I'll take my stand,
To live and die in Dixie;
Away, away, away down south in Dixie,
Away, away away down south in Dixie.

DANIEL DECATUR EMMETT (1818–1904)
Arranged by Maxwell Eckstein

Battle Hymn of the Republic

Mine eyes have seen the glory of the coming of the Lord;
He is trampling out the vintage where the grapes of wrath are stored;
He hath loosed the fateful lightning of His terrible swift sword:
His truth is marching on.

Chorus
    Glory, glory, hallelujah!
    Glory, glory, hallelujah!
    Glory, glory, hallelujah!
    His truth is marching on.

He has sounded forth the trumpet that shall never call retreat;
He is sifting out the hearts of men before his judgment seat.
Oh, be swift, my soul, to answer Him! Be jubilant, my feet!
Our God is marching on.

(Julia Ward Howe)

T. E. BISHOP
Arranged by Maxwell Eckstein

Arkansas Traveler

American Folk Tune
Arranged by Maxwell Eckstein

Carry Me Back To Old Virginny

Carry me back to old Virginny;
There's where the cotton and the corn and 'tatoes grow.
There's where the birds warble sweet in the springtime.
There's where this old darky's heart am longed to go.
There's where I labored so hard for old Massa,
Day after day in the field of yellow corn.
No place on earth do I love more sincerely
Than old Virginny, the state where I was born.

JAMES A. BLAND
Arranged by Maxwell Eckstein

Turkey In The Straw

Allegro moderato

American Folk Tune
Arranged by Maxwell Eckstein

Home on the Range

Oh, give me a home where the buffalo roam,
Where the deer and the antelope play,
Where seldom is heard a discouraging word
And the skies are not cloudy all day.

Refrain

Home, home on the range,
Where the deer and the antelope play,
Where seldom is heard a discouraging word
And the skies are not cloudy all day.

American Cowboy Song
Arranged by Maxwell Eckstein

The Old Oaken Bucket

How dear to my heart are the scenes of my childhood,
When fond recollection presents them to view!
The orchard, the meadow, the deep tangled wildwood,
And every loved spot which my infancy knew.

The wide spreading pond, and the mill that stood by it,
The bridge and the rock where the cataract fell;
The cot of my father, the dairy house nigh it,
And e'en the rude bucket that hung in the well.

Chorus
The old oaken bucket, the iron-bound bucket,
The moss-covered bucket that hung in the well.
(S. Woodworth)

C. KIALLMARK
Arranged by Maxwell Eckstein

I'll Take You Home Again, Kathleen

I'll take you home again, Kathleen,
Across the ocean wild and wide,
To where your heart has ever been,
Since first you were my bonnie bride.
The roses all have left your cheek,
I've watched them fade and die;
Your voice is sad whene'er you speak,
And tears bedim your loving eyes.

Chorus

Oh! I will take you back again,
To where your heart will feel no pain,
And when the fields are fresh and green,
I'll take you to your home again.

T. P. WESTENDORF
Arranged by Maxwell Eckstein

Home, Sweet Home

'Mid pleasures and palaces though we may roam,
Be it ever so humble, there's no place like home;
A charm from the skies seems to hallow us there,
Which, seek through the world, is ne'er met with elsewhere.
Home! Home! Sweet, sweet home,
There's no place like home,
There's no place like home!
(John Howard Payne)

HENRY R. BISHOP (1786-1855)
Arranged by Maxwell Eckstein

Long, Long Ago

Tell me the tales that to me were so dear,
Long, long ago, Long, long ago,
Sing me the songs I delighted to hear,
Long, long ago, Long ago.
Now you are come, all my grief is removed,
Let me forget that so long you have roved.
Let me believe that you love as you loved,
Long, long ago, Long ago.

THOMAS H. BAYLY (1797-1839)
Arranged by Maxwell Eckstein

Love's Old Sweet Song

Just a song at twilight, when the lights are low,
And the flick'ring shadows softly come and go,
Tho the heart be weary, sad the day and long,
Still to us at twilight comes love's old song,
Comes love's old sweet song.

JAMES LYMAN MOLLOY (1837-1909)
Arranged by Maxwell Eckstein

Silver Threads Among the Gold

Darling, I am growing old;
Silver threads among the gold
Shine upon my brow to-day;
Life is fading fast away.
But, my darling, you will be, will be
Always young and fair to me,
Yes, my darling, you will be
Always young and fair to me.

Chorus

Darling, I am growing old;
Silver threads among the gold
Shine upon my brow to-day;
Life is fading fast away.

H. P. DANKS (1834 - 1903)
Arranged by Maxwell Eckstein

Oh, My Darling Clementine

In a cavern in a canyon,
Excavating for a mine,
Dwelt a miner, forty niner,
And his daughter Clementine.

Refrain
Oh, my darling, Oh, my darling,
Oh, my darling Clementine,
You are lost and gone forever,
Dreadful sorry, Clementine.

P. MONTROSE
Arranged by Maxwell Eckstein

Oh! Susanna

I came from Alabama
Wid my banjo on my knee,
I'm gwine to Lousiana,
My true love for to see.
It rained all night de day I left,
De weather it was dry,
De sun so hot I froze to death;
Susanna, don't you cry.

Chorus
Oh, Susanna,
Oh, don't you cry for me,
I've come from Alabama
Wid my banjo on my knee.

STEPHEN C. FOSTER (1826-1864)
Arranged by Maxwell Eckstein

My Old Kentucky Home

The sun shines bright in the old Kentucky home,
'Tis summer, the darkies are gay;
The corn-top's ripe and the meadow's in the bloom,
While the birds make music all the day.

The young folks roll on the little cabin floor,
All merry, all happy and bright;
By 'n' by hard times comes a-knocking at the door,
Then my old Kentucky home, good night!

Refrain
Weep no more, my lady, O weep no more to-day!
We will sing one song for the old Kentucky home,
For the old Kentucky home far away.

STEPHEN C. FOSTER (1826-1864)
Arranged by Maxwell Eckstein

Old Folks At Home

'Way down upon de Swanee ribber,
Far, far away,
Dere's wha my heart is turning ebber,
Dere's wha de old folks stay.
All up and down de whole creation,
Sadly I roam,
Still longing for de old plantation,
And for de old folks at home.

Chorus
All de world am sad and dreary,
Eb'rywhere I roam.
Oh, darkies, how my heart grows weary,
Far from de old folks at home.

STEPHEN C. FOSTER (1826-1864)
Arranged by Maxwell Eckstein

Beautiful Dreamer

Beautiful dreamer, wake unto me.
Starlight and dewdrops are waiting for thee,
Sounds of the rude world heard in the day,
Lulled by the moonlight, have all passed away.
Beautiful dreamer, queen of my song,
List while I woo thee with soft melody;
Gone are the cares of life's busy throng.
Beautiful dreamer, awake unto me,
Beautiful dreamer, awake unto me.

STEPHEN C. FOSTER (1826-1864)
Arranged by Maxwell Eckstein

Jeanie With the Light Brown Hair

I dream of Jeanie with the light brown hair
Borne, like a vapor, on the summer air;
I see her tripping where the bright streams play,
Happy as the daisies that dance on her way.
Many were the wild notes her merry voice would pour,
Many were the blithe birds that warbled them o'er.
Oh! I dream of Jeanie with the light brown hair
Floating, like a vapor, on the soft summer air.

STEPHEN C. FOSTER (1826-1864)
Arranged by Maxwell Eckstein

Old Black Joe

Gone are the days when my heart was young and gay;
Gone are my friends from the cotton fields away;
Gone from the earth to a better land, I know,
I hear their gentle voices calling,
"Old Black Joe!"

Chorus
I'm coming, I'm coming,
For my head is bending low;
I hear those gentle voices calling,
"Old Black Joe!"

STEPHEN C. FOSTER (1826-1864)
Arranged by Maxwell Eckstein

Swing Low, Sweet Chariot

Swing low, sweet chariot,
Comin' fo' to carry me home,
Swing low, sweet chariot,
Comin' fo' to carry me home.

I looked over Jordan and what did I see,
Comin' fo' to carry me home?
A band of angels comin' after me,
Comin' fo' to carry me home.

If you get there before I do,
Comin' fo' to carry me home,
Tell all my friends I'm comin' too,
Comin' fo' to carry me home.

Negro Spiritual
Arranged by Maxwell Eckstein

Short'nin' Bread

Put on de skillet, Put on de led;
Mammy's gwine to make a li'l' short'nin' bread.
Dat ain't all she's gwine to do,
She's gwine to make a little coffee too.

Chorus
Mammy's li'l' baby loves short'nin', short'nin,'
Mammy's li'l' baby loves short'nin' bread.

Southern Mountain Tune
(American)
Arranged by Maxwell Eckstein

Drink To Me Only With Thine Eyes

Drink to me only with thine eyes, and I will pledge with mine;
Or leave a kiss within the cup,
And I'll not ask for wine;
The thirst that from the soul doth rise
Doth ask a drink divine;
But might I of Jove's nectar sip,
I would not change for thine.

I sent thee late a rosy wreath, not so much hon'ring thee
As giving it a hope that there
It could not withered be;
But thou thereon didst only breathe,
And sent'st it back to me,
Since when it grows and smells, I swear,
Not of itself, but thee.

(Ben Jonson)

Old English Air
Arranged by Maxwell Eckstein

Country Gardens
(HANDKERCHIEF DANCE)

Traditional Morris Dance Tune
Arranged by Maxwell Eckstein

Pop Goes The Weasel

O, all around the chicken coop,
The monkey chased the weasel,
And that's the way the money goes.
Pop! Goes the weasel.
I've no time to wait or sigh,
No time to wheedle,
Only time to say good-bye,
Pop! Goes the weasel.

Traditional American
Arranged by Maxwell Eckstein

Three Blind Mice

Three blind mice,
Three blind mice,
See how they run!
See how they run!
They all ran after the farmer's wife,
She cut off their tails with a carving knife,
Did you ever see such a sight in your life
As three blind mice.

Round
Arranged by Maxwell Eckstein

Polly Wolly Doodle

Oh, I went down south for to see my Sal,
Sing Polly Wolly Doodle all the day;
My Sally am a spunky gal,
Sing Polly Wolly Doodle all the day.
Fare thee well, fare thee well,
Fare thee well my fairy fay,
For I'm going to Louisiana,
For to see my Susyanna,
Sing Polly Wolly Doodle all the day.

College Song
Arranged by Maxwell Eckstein

The Lost Chord

Seated one day at the organ
I was weary and ill at ease;
And my fingers wandered idly
Over the noisy keys.

I know not what I was playing;
Or what I was dreaming then,
But I struck one chord of music,
Like the sound of a great Amen.

(Adelaide A. Proctor)

Sir ARTHUR SULLIVAN (1842-1900)
Arranged by Maxwell Eckstein

We Sail The Ocean Blue
(H. M. S. Pinafore)

We sail the ocean blue,
And our saucy ship's a beauty;
We're sober men and true,
And attentive to our duty.
When the balls whistle free o'er the bright blue sea
We stand to our guns all day.
When at anchor we ride
On the Portsmouth tide
We've plenty of time for play, Ahoy! Ahoy!
Ahoy! Ahoy!
We stand to our guns, to our guns all day.
We sail the ocean blue,
And our saucy ship's a beauty;
We're sober men and true,
And attentive to our duty;
Our saucy ship's a beauty,
We're attentive to our duty,
We're sober men and true,
We sail the ocean blue.

GILBERT and SULLIVAN
(1836-1911)　(1842-1900)
Arranged by Maxwell Eckstein

I'm Called Little Buttercup
(H.M.S. Pinafore)

I'm called little Buttercup,
Dear little Buttercup,
Though I could never tell why;
But still I'm called Buttercup,
Poor little Buttercup,
Sweet little Buttercup, I.
I've snuff and tobaccy,
And excellent jacky;
I've scissors, and watches, and knives;
I've ribbons and laces
To set off the faces
Of pretty young sweethearts and wives,
I've treacle and toffee,
I've tea and I've coffee.
Soft tommy and succulent chops;
I've chickens and conies,
And pretty polonies,
And excellent peppermint drops.
Then buy of your Buttercup,
Dear little Buttercup,
Sailors should never be shy,
So buy of your Buttercup,
Poor little Buttercup,
Come, of your Buttercup buy.

GILBERT and SULLIVAN
(1836-1911)   (1842-1900)
Arranged by Maxwell Eckstein

I am the Captain of the "Pinafore"
(H.M.S. Pinafore)

(Captain) I am the captain of the "Pinafore,"
(Chorus) And a right good captain too!
(Captain) You're very, very good,
And be it understood, I command a right good crew.
(Chorus) We're very, very good,
And be it understood,
He commands a right good crew.
(Captain) Tho related to a peer,
I can hand, reef, and steer,
Or ship a selvagee;
I am never known to quail
At the fury of a gale,
And I'm never, never sick at sea.
(Chorus) What, never?
(Captain) No, never!
(Chorus) What, never?
(Captain) Well, hardly ever,
(Chorus) He's hardly ever sick at sea.
Then give three cheers, and one cheer more,
For the hardy captain of the "Pinafore"!
Then give three cheers, and one cheer more,
For the captain of the "Pinafore."

GILBERT and SULLIVAN
(1836-1911) (1842-1900)
Arranged by Maxwell Eckstein

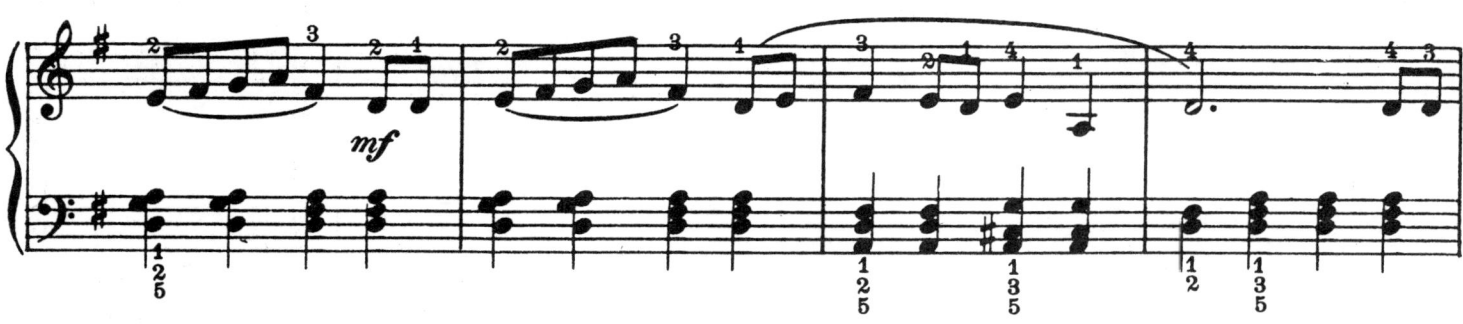

The Flowers That Bloom in the Spring
(The Mikado)

The flowers that bloom in the spring, Tra la,
Breathe promise of merry sunshine—
As we merrily dance and we sing, Tra la
We welcome the hope that they bring, Tra la,
Of a summer of roses and wine,
Of a summer of roses and wine.
And that's what we mean when we say that a thing
Is welcome as flowers that bloom in the spring.
Tra la la la la,— Tra la la la la—
The flowers that bloom in the spring.

GILBERT and SULLIVAN
(1836-1911)   (1842-1900)
Arranged by Maxwell Eckstein

Tit-Willow
(The Mikado)

On a tree by a river a little tom-tit
Sang, "Willow, tit-willow, tit-willow!"
And I said to him, Dicky-bird, why do you sit
Singing, 'Willow, tit-willow, tit-willow'?
"Is it weakness of intellect, birdie?" I cried,
"Or a rather tough worm in your little inside?"
With a shake of his poor little head, he replied,
"Oh, willow, tit-willow, tit-willow!"

GILBERT and SULLIVAN
(1836-1911) (1842-1900)
Arranged by Maxwell Eckstein

El Choclo
Argentine Tango

A.G. VILLOLDO
Arranged by Maxwell Eckstein

Juanita

Soft o'er the fountain,
Ling'ring falls the southern moon;
Far o'er the mountain,
Breaks the day too soon!
In thy dark eyes' splendor,
Where the warm light loves to dwell,
Weary looks, yet tender,
Speak their fond farewell.

Nita! Juanita! Ask thy soul if we should part!
Nita! Juanita! Lean thou on my heart.

Spanish Air
Arranged by Maxwell Eckstein

Beautiful Heaven
(Cielito Lindo)

1. With all your smiles
   And your pretty wiles,
   And those dimples, Cielito Lindo,
   You bewitch every one of us,
   Little sweetheart, Cielito Lindo!

   Refrain
   Ay, ay, ay, ay, Cielito Lindo,
   Tis cupid's dart
   That has pierced my heart,
   And I'll win you, Cielito Lindo!

2. On one and all
   Let your glances fall,
   While we're dancing, Cielito Lindo,
   But I vow I shall be the one
   Who will win you, Cielito Lindo!

(Susanna Myers) *Arranged by Maxwell Eckstein*

La Cucaracha

La cucaracha, la cucaracha,
Ya no puede caminar,
Por que no tiene, por que le falta,
Marihuana que fumar,
La cucamar.
Un pan a de rofue amisa,
No en contrando que rezar.

Le pidio ala Virgen pura,
Dinero para gastar;
La cucaracha, la cucaracha,
Ya no puede caminar,
Por que no tiene, por que le falta,
Marihuana que fumar.

Mexican Folk-Song
Arranged by Maxwell Eckstein

Auld Lang Syne

Should auld acquaintance be forgot,
And never brought to mind?
Should auld acquaintance be forgot,
And days of auld lang syne?

For auld lang syne, my dear,
For auld lang syne;
We'll tak' a cup o' kindness yet
For auld lang syne.

Scottish Song
Arranged by Maxwell Eckstein

Blue Bells of Scotland

Oh! where, tell me, where is your Highland laddie gone?
Oh! where, tell me, where is your Highland laddie gone?
He's gone with streaming banners where noble deeds are done,
And my sad heart will tremble till he comes safely home.

Oh! where, tell me, where did your Highland laddie dwell?
Oh! where, tell me, where did your Highland laddie dwell?
He dwelt in bonnie Scotland where blooms the sweet blue bell;
And it's oh! in my heart, that I love my laddie well.

Scottish Air
Arranged by Maxwell Eckstein

Annie Laurie

Maxwelton's braes are bonnie,
Where early fa's the dew,
And 'twas there that Annie Laurie
Gave me her promise true;
Gave me her promise true,
Which ne'er forgot will be,
And for bonnie Annie Laurie
I'd lay me doon and dee.
(William Douglas)

LADY JOHN SCOTT (1810-1900)
Arranged by Maxwell Eckstein

Andante moderato

Comin' Thro' The Rye

If a body meet a body
Comin' thro' the rye,
If a body kiss a body,
Need a body cry?
Every lassie has her laddie,
Nane they say ha'e I;
Yet a' the lads they smile on me,
When comin' thro' the rye.
(Anonymous, altered by Robert Burns)

Scottish Air
Arranged by Maxwell Eckstein

Londonderry Air

Would God I were the tender apple blossom
That floats and falls from off the twisted bough,
To lie and faint within your silken bosom,
Within your silken bosom as that does now!
Or would I were a little burnished apple
For you to pluck me, gliding by so cold,
While sun and shade your robe of lawn will dapple,
Your robe of lawn and your hair's spun gold.

Irish Folk Tune
Arranged by Maxwell Eckstein

The Last Rose Of Summer

'Tis the last rose of summer
Left blooming alone;
All her lovely companions
Are faded and gone;
No flow'r of her kindred,
No rosebud is nigh
To reflect back her blushes,
Or give sigh for sigh.
　　　　　(Thomas Moore)

Old Irish Air
"The Groves of Blarney"
Arranged by Maxwell Eckstein

None But The Lonely Heart

None but the lonely heart can know my sadness;
Alone, and parted far from joy and gladness.
Heav'n's boundless arch I see spread out above me.
Ah; what a distance drear to one who loves me!
None but the lonely heart can know my sadness,
Alone and parted far from joy and gladness,
Alone, and parted far from joy and gladness,
My senses fail, a burning fire devours me.
None but the lonely heart can know my sadness.

(English version by Arthur Westbrook)

P. I. TSCHAIKOWSKY (1840-1893)
Arranged by Maxwell Eckstein

Two Guitars

Russian Gipsy Song
Arranged by Maxwell Eckstein

A Song of India

The diamonds in their rocky caves are countless,
And countless are the pearls in southern oceans,
The glory of distant India's realm.
In these glowing oceans;
In a ruddy sapphire;
Sitteth there the Phoenix,
Bird with maiden's features,
Paradise - like singing

Softly from her floweth;
She her radiant feathers
O'er the ocean draweth.
He who hears her singing
Mem'ry no more knoweth.
The diamonds in their rocky caves are countless,
And countless are the pearls in southern oceans,
The glory of distant India's realm.

(English version by George Harris, Jr.)

N. RIMSKY KORSAKOFF (1844-1908)
Arranged by Maxwell Eckstein

Dark Eyes

Russian Folk-Song
Arranged by Maxwell Eckstein

Song of the Volga Boatmen

Yo, heave, ho!
Yo, heave, ho!
Once again we sing
Yo, heave, ho!
Yo, heave, ho!
Yo, heave, ho!
Once again we sing

Yo, heave, ho!
While we drag the barge along,
Cheer our toil with the Volga song.
Ai, da-da, ai da,
Ai, da-da, ai da,
Once again we sing
Yo, heave, ho!

(Translated by Susanna Myers)

Russian Folk Song
Arranged by Maxwell Eckstein

Melody in F

ANTON RUBINSTEIN (1830–1894)
Arranged by Maxwell Eckstein

Moderato

THEME FROM
Marche Slave

P. TSCHAIKOWSKY (1840-1893)
Arranged by Maxwell Eckstein

The Merry Widow
WALTZ

FRANZ LEHAR
Arranged by Maxwell Eckstein

Tales From The Vienna Woods
WALTZ

JOHANN STRAUSS, Jr. (1825-1899)
Arranged by Maxwell Eckstein

Blue Danube
WALTZ

JOHANN STRAUSS, Jr. (1825-1899)
Arranged by Maxwell Eckstein

Nearer, My God, To Thee

Nearer, my God, to Thee, Nearer to Thee;
E'en though it be a cross
That raiseth me.
Still all my song shall be,
Nearer, my God, to Thee,
Nearer, my God, to Thee,
Nearer to Thee.
(Sarah F. Adams)

LOWELL MASON (1792-1872)
Arranged by Maxwell Eckstein

Rock Of Ages

Rock of Ages, cleft for me,
Let me hide myself in Thee;
Let the water and the blood,
From Thy wounded side that flowed,
Be of sin the double cure,
Save from wrath and make me pure.

While I draw this fleeting breath,
When my eyes shall close in death,
When I rise to worlds unknown,
And behold Thee on Thy throne,
Rock of Ages, cleft for me,
Let me hide myself in Thee
(A.M. Toplady)

THOMAS HASTINGS (1787-1872)
Arranged by Maxwell Eckstein

Adeste Fideles
(O Come, All ye Faithful)

O come, all ye faithful,
Joyful and triumphant,
O come ye, O come ye to Bethlehem.
Come and behold Him,
Born the king of angels:
O come, let us adore Him,
O come, let us adore Him,
O come, let us adore Him,
Christ the Lord.

JOHN READING (? - 1692)
Arranged by Maxwell Eckstein

Silent Night

Silent night! Holy night!
All is calm, all is bright.
'Round yon virgin mother and Child!
Holy Infant, so tender and mild,
Sleep in heavenly peace,
Sleep in heavenly peace.

(Joseph Mohr)

FRANZ GRUBER
Arranged by Maxwell Eckstein

La Donna e mobile
(Rigoletto)

Woman is changeable, Light as a feather,
False as fair weather, Who can believe her?
Al-ways a beautiful face so beguiling,
Weeping or smiling, Is a deceiver!
Woman, ah, woman!
Light as a feather,
False as fair weather, Who can believe?
Who can believe?
Ah, who can believe?

G. VERDI (1813–1901)
Arranged by Maxwell Eckstein

Ave Maria

Ave Maria! Maiden mild!
Listen to a maiden's prayer,
For Thou canst hear though from the wild,
Thou canst save amid despair.
Safe may we sleep beneath Thy care,
Though banished, outcast and reviled.
O Maiden, hear a maiden's prayer
O Mother, hear a suppliant child!
Ave Maria!

(Walter Scott)

FRANZ SCHUBERT (1797–1828)
Arranged by Maxwell Eckstein

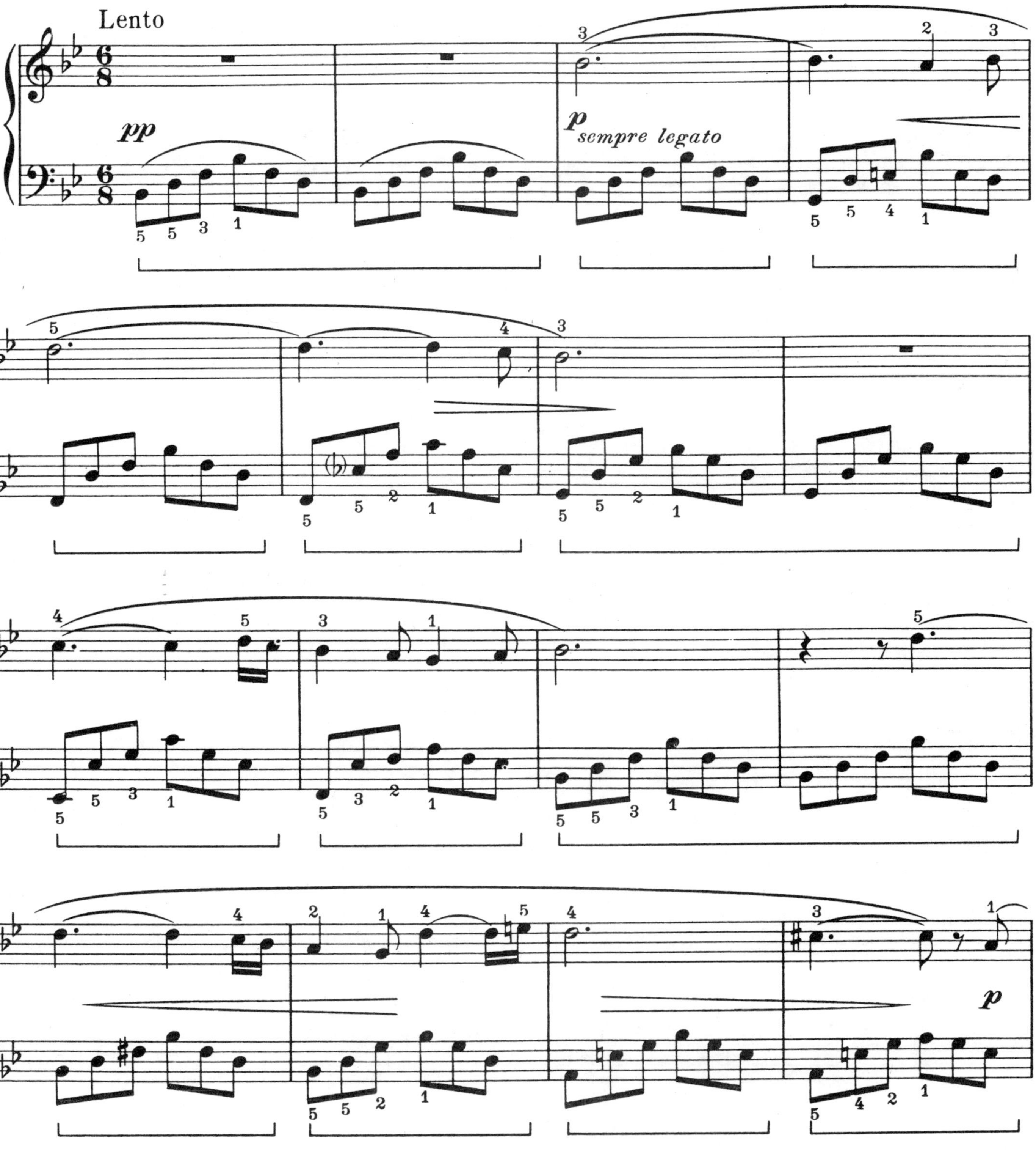

Liebesträume
Theme from
LOVE DREAMS

FRANZ LISZT (1811-1886)
Arranged by Maxwell Eckstein

Serenade

Softly through the night is calling,
Love, my song to thee.
Shades of night are swiftly falling,
Dearest, come to me!

In the moonlight gently swaying,
Whisp'ring leaves I hear;
"No one listens," they are saying,
"Fair one, do not fear."

(English version by Alice Mattullath)

FRANZ SCHUBERT (1797-1828)
Arranged by Maxwell Eckstein

Cradle Song
(Lullaby)

Go to sleep now, dear love, 'neath roses above;
Sweet blossoms white and red shall bloom by thy bed.
When the dawn lights the skies, open wide thy dear eyes,
When the dawn lights the skies, open wide thy dear eyes.

Little angels will keep their watch o'er thy sleep;
In dreams thou shalt see a fair Christmas tree,
And in paradise rove, with the angels above,
And in paradise rove, with the angels above.

(English version by Alice Mattullath)

JOHANNES BRAHMS (1833–1897)
Arranged by Maxwell Eckstein

Aloha Oe!
Hawaiian Song of Farewell

Proudly sweeps the rainbow o'er the cliff,
Borne swiftly by the western gale,
While the song of lover's parting grief,
Sadly echoes amid the flow'ring vale.

Chorus
Farewell to thee, farewell to thee!
The winds will carry back my sad refrain;
One fond embrace before good-bye,
Farewell until we meet again.

QUEEN LILIUOKALANI
Arranged by Maxwell Eckstein

Humoresque

ANTON DVOŘÁK (1841-1904)
Arranged by Maxwell Eckstein

Poco lento e grazioso

Songs My Mother Taught Me

Songs my mother taught me
In the days long vanished;
Seldom from her eyelids
Were the tear-drops banished.
Now I teach my children
Each melodious measure;
Oft the tears are flowing,
Oft they flow from my mem'ry's treasure.

ANTON DVOŘÁK (1841-1904)
Arranged by Maxwell Eckstein

The Old Refrain

I often think of home, Dee-oo-lee-ay,
When I am all alone and far away:
I sing an old refrain: Dee-oo-lee-ay,
For it recalls to me a bygone day.
It takes me back again to meadows fair,
Where sunlight's golden rays beam everywhere,
My childhood joys again come back to me,
My mother's face in fancy, too, I see,
It was my mother taught me how to sing
And to that memory my heart will cling,
I'm never sad and lone while on my way
As long as I can sing: Dee-oo-lee-ay!*

(Alice Mattullath)

Viennese Melody
Arranged by Maxwell Eckstein

* Included by permission of Charles Foley

Stein Song
(University of Maine)

Fill the steins to dear old Maine,
Shout till the rafters ring!
Stand and drink a toast once again!
Let every loyal Maine man sing.
(Then) Drink to all the happy hours,
Drink to the careless days,
Drink to Maine, our Alma Mater,
The college of our hearts always.

To the trees, to the sky!
To the spring in its glorious happiness,
To the youth, to the fire,
To the life that is moving and calling us!
To the gods, to the Fates,
To the rulers of men and their destinies;
To the lips, to the eyes,
To the girls who will love us some day!

E. A. FENSTAD
Arranged by Maxwell Eckstein

O Sole Mio
(My Sun)

Behold the brilliant sun in all its splendor,
Forgotten is the storm, the clouds now vanish,
The fresh'ning breezes heavy airs will banish;
Behold the brilliant sun in all its splendor!

Chorus

A sun I know of that's brighter still,
This sun, so radiant, is naught but thee,
Thy face so fair to see,
That shall now my sun forever be!

E. DI CAPUA
Arranged by Maxwell Eckstein

Poem
("My Moonlight Madonna")

Where are you, beautiful moonlight Madonna?
Like the dew you're gone with the dawn, Madonna,
Leaving clues on the carpets of evening,
Footprints of magical weaving,
Tracing the path of my moonlight Madonna.
Kneeling under the heavenly ceiling
I pray, to heaven appealing
For her return with the moonlight upon her,
For the return of my moonlight Madonna.
(Paul Francis Webster)

ZDENKO FIBICH
Arranged by Maxwell Eckstein

La Marseillaise
French National Anthem

Ye sons of France, awake to glory!
Hark, hark, what myriads bid you rise!
Your children, wives, and grandsires hoary,
Behold their tears and hear their cries!
Behold their tears and hear their cries!
Shall hateful tyrants, mischief breeding,
With hireling hosts, a ruffian band,
Affright and desolate the land,
While peace and liberty lie bleeding?

To arms, to arms, ye brave!
Th'avenging sword unsheathed!
March on, march on, all hearts resolved
On victory or death.

C. J. ROUGET DE L'ISLE (1760-1836)
Arranged by Maxwell Eckstein

CLASSIFIED INDEX

PATRIOTIC MELODIES
America	5
America, the Beautiful	6
Battle Hymn of the Republic	12
Dixie Land	10
Star-Spangled Banner, The	8
Yankee Doodle	9

AMERICAN FOLK TUNES
Arkansas Traveler	13
Carry Me Back to Old Virginny	14
Home on the Range	18
Turkey in the Straw	16

HOME and HEART MELODIES
Home, Sweet Home	22
I'll Take You Home Again, Kathleen	20
Long, Long Ago	24
Love's Old Sweet Song	25
Oh, My Darling Clementine	28
Old Oaken Bucket	19
Silver Threads Among the Gold	26

STEPHEN FOSTER WORKS
Beautiful Dreamer	33
Jeanie with the Light Brown Hair	34
My Old Kentucky Home	30
Oh! Susanna	29
Old Black Joe	35
Old Folks at Home	32

NEGRO SPIRITUALS
Short'nin' Bread	38
Swing Low, Sweet Chariot	36

ENGLISH TUNES and AIRS
Country Gardens	40
Drink to Me Only with Thine Eyes	39
Lost Chord, The	45
Polly Wolly Doodle	44
Pop Goes the Weasel	42
Three Blind Mice	43

ECHOES from GILBERT & SULLIVAN
Flowers That Bloom in the Spring, The	52
I Am the Captain of the Pinafore	50
I'm Called Little Buttercup	48
Tit-Willow	53
We Sail the Ocean Blue	46

SPANISH FOLK TUNES
Beautiful Heaven	57
El Choclo	54
Juanita	56
La Cucaracha	58

SCOTCH FOLK TUNES
Annie Laurie	61
Auld Lang Syne	59
Blue Bells of Scotland, The	60
Comin' Thro' the Rye	62

IRISH FOLK TUNES
Last Rose of Summer, The	64
Londonderry Air	63

RUSSIAN FOLK TUNES and COMPOSITIONS by Russian Composers
Dark Eyes	72
Marche Slave (Tschaikowsky)	76
Melody in F (Rubinstein)	74
None But the Lonely Heart (Tschaikowsky)	66
Song of India, A (Rimsky-Korsakoff)	70
Volga Boatmen, Song of the	73
Two Guitars	68

CELEBRATED WALTZES
Blue Danube	80
Merry Widow, The	77
Tales from the Vienna Woods	78

OPERATIC EXCERPTS
La Donna e mobile (Rigoletto)	86
Merry Widow, The	77

HYMNS
Adeste Fideles	84
Nearer My God to Thee	82
Rock of Ages	83
Silent Night	85

COMPOSITIONS from the MASTERS
Ave Maria (Schubert)	87
Cradle Song (Brahms)	96
Humoresque (Dvorak)	98
Liebesträume (Liszt)	92
Marche Slave (Tschaikowsky)	76
Melody in F (Rubinstein)	74
None But the Lonely Heart (Tschaikowsky)	66
Serenade (Schubert)	94
Song of India, A (Rimsky-Korsakoff)	70
Songs My Mother Taught Me (Dvorak)	100
Who Is Sylvia? (Schubert)	90

MISCELLANEOUS
Aloha Oe! (Hawaiian)	97
La Marseillaise (French)	110
Old Refrain, The (Viennese)	102
O Sole Mio (Capua)	106
Poem (Fibich)	108
Stein Song	104